AURORAS OVER ACADIA

AURORAS OVER ACADIA

PAUL LIEBOW

Paul A Liebow

For Geri

Thank you!!!
for your help
and concern
for PTSD
sufferers

atmosphere press

Sept. 2019

TABLE OF CONTENTS

39 / Ice on Fire

Dedicated to my Mom and Dad

My father Averill arrived at Ellis Island as a little 8year old Jewish boy fleeing the Nazis. He became a Lieutenant Colonel in our Medical Corps during WW II, and lead pathologist on The *Atomic Bomb Casualty Commission.*

Thirty years later he went back to Germany with the US Army civilian protocol rank of Second Star General. He was widely loved as an outstandingly skilled and caring teacher. The *Liebow Auditorium* is named in his honor.

My mother Carolyn made it all possible. She was a nurse and Captain in my Dad's Yale Unit. She returned home, took off her Army uniform, and made our loving home in rural Connecticut.

Maine on My Mind

1 / Maine on My Mind

Auroras over Acadia

I love the Aurora when it's low
on my far horizon, faintly gleaming,
like the cloud city which I know will
quench the nostalgia of Arctic dreaming.

I love its cool green glowing dance,
a churning river of metal and crystal,
and when it's a warm red waterfall,
aftermath of love and home fires burning.

I love the Aurora's pulsing rhythm,
like the sound of a glass harmonica,
swaying with the Sun as it vibrates
like a transparent bell in a hymn.

I love the Aurora most of all
when it streams down slowly
from the highest altar of sky,
in a swirling twirling dance

of rainbows within rainbows,
on the walls of the circus tent
where we lie on our backs
side by side in our dreams.

THE ISLAND

Come walk with me in misty time
on Cranberry Isle by the shining sea.
Our everyday worlds will morph sublime
as a spotty dog dances down a path of mine.

Mushrooms sway in the moonlit breeze,
ferns nod their other-worldly knowing,
wood sprites gather 'round our knees
to guide our green-eyed ghostly going.

Talking deer lie under breathing trees,
sipping night's nectar off the leaves.
Painted birds sway and dance in lines,
twittering their secrets in nursery rhymes.

So sit with me in the interstices
of silence and slow time.
Wade barefoot with me in reality
as we meld into our universal we.

A Cranberry Island Trilogy

I. The Tide Pool

The Tide Pool lay cradled in the island's arms
and my first job was to wake up before dawn
and row up and across it on an ebbing tide

to dig clams for B & B, until it flooded back in.
$23 dollars a bushel was a big deal in those days
and some lucky days I had almost a bushel.

I hovered over *lobster holes* deep in the glacial clay
where the little ones hid out in their little caves—
saw only claw tips tapping and antennae waving.

Gulls chortled way out on the morning rocks,
ospreys and eagles swooped out of the marsh,
the Sun set in *sky-blue-pink* if rain was coming.

We watched the Moon rise over the Eastern Way,
floating silently on the flood tide back into the Pool,
faster than I could row my Whitehall skiff against it.

Seals spy-hopped in the moonbeams,
so close we could look into their eyes,
hear them breathing and even smell them.

Meteor showers of mackerel chased herring
brit through their phosphorescent gleaming,
deep in the dark of the August moon.

II. The Great Heath

The Great Heath was the island's Heart
of Darkness, where the old-timers said
a whole team of oxen once sunk out of sight
so far they couldn't even save their meat.

We wandered out on it one afternoon
as a wave of wet fog snuck quietly in.
Suddenly it all looked the same to us
in every direction, bordered by stunted

skunk pines, gradually getting larger
as they rose up out of the nacreous bog.
We wandered for hours on its wet back
of bouncing peat and emerged shaking.

Years later Allison, a crusty old islander,
showed us tiny fragile pink orchids
and other minute treasures hiding
among pitcher plants and sundew.

The island was only 800 acres and inhabited,
but it still looms enormous in my mind.
Close contact with plant and animal beings,
the intensity of the elements, the stillness

and my utter absorption in the moment
still flood me with intense emotions,
in the far more primeval sense
I usually feel out in true wilderness.

III. The Back Shore

The Back Shore was another world,
where we sat at night by a driftwood
fire and heard our ghosts laughing
and dancing in *thickafog* just above us.

We camped on Mermaids' Egg Beach,
watched the huge pink granite eggs
rumble round and smooth in the surf,
saw sunspots floating on a rosehip sun

lolled back in the huge crash of waves
sweeping in from an offshore hurricane,
saw the Moon dart out of the *cloud massif*
as the storm swept off east to Nova Scotia.

We watched massed rafts of sea ducks
resting far out on the October horizon,
first flapping up at dusk, one after another,
then sinking back again, until suddenly

they all rose up together and flew south
on the great miracle of migration.

ROWING

If you were a summer kid from away
you could row any way you wanted to,
but it was always looking over your shoulder
and orbiting the handles around each other,
in a great big hurry to impress the girls.

For an islander there was only one way to row—
as you'd always done, just like your father,
when life on the sea was a timeless meditation,
but no one would ever have admitted meditating.

Filmore on the back seat of a tiny two-seater dinghy,
pushing it forward with the oars instead of pulling

Charlie swishing one oar from a punt's stern seat,
leaning back and forth like a Venetian gondolier

Tudd standing high on the front seat pulling one oar
to both sides, his pipe upside down in his smile

Pink Stanley in his huge old high-sided dory—
standing high up, looking down into the big empty
square tower of its inboard outboard motor well

stooping way over to push the huge oars forward,
then straightening his back out later by pulling it
in over the flats like a modern-day Volga boatman.

ANGEL IN A PEAR TREE
painting by artist Carl Nelson

Carl was a huge huggable stuffed toy bear,
in his great big baggy and painty shorts,
faded yellow and black striped rugby jersey
and big flat floppy sneakers without socks.

Thick hair on his neck and chest and legs
stood out proudly, bushy and wafting in white
on his Magical Disney Bee striped body.
Tufted scalp hair twirled into twin antennae.

His short gnarly legs and knobby knees were
so bent and bowed, a caricature of a cowboy's,
that you could even imagine pollen baskets
hanging on his ankles as he shuffled by.

Carl painted the most beautiful birch
and spruce and flowers in fractal planes,
as perfectly arranged in visual concert
as any Monet, Redon or Van Gogh.

My Dad so loved Carl's painting of *shadblow*—
fluttering white *saskatoon* or sugarplum petals—
that he could still lovingly say *Angel in a Pear Tree!*
long after a stroke garbled his speech forever.

Carl's great stooped shoulders stooped even more
after he had both collarbones broken in a mugging.
He moved back to his gray Great Cranberry cottage
that lived in his eclectic garden he named *Tosh Park*

Forever

PETER

Peter was a gaunt shadow creeping past
our delirious nights of hide and seek,
or sometimes just a bottle breaking
somewhere back deep in the alders

—still clambering around his golden youth
in his old rolling-over Eastport *pinky sloop*,
its timbers springing from the bow beam
like little shark mouths out of the surf.

Its huge old rusty anchor still salutes us
from the oil rainbows shining in a puddle
on top of a great gray glacial boulder,
and battery acid streaked brown grass.

His big square house just up *The Lane*
was lit only by a few faint orange fingers—
flickering fire in an old wood stove,
and the mysterious flutterings of an old oil lantern.

Peter always walked wistfully leaning forward
with his big rum bottle bulging under his coat—
his only words usually just a jaunty *Hi-yah!*
—unless he was asleep in his comfy bed

in the back of someone's pickup truck.

CARL

I thought Carl was the biggest, strongest,
meanest, scariest man in all the World
until I went out to California and saw real
Hell's Angels flying in gangs by the Pacific.

He drove a big black flatbed pick-up truck,
smiling devil's head and double dice on the hood.
He shot pigeons and crows in his front yard
and flies high on the kitchen wall with his .22

being very careful not to hit his Mom at work—
postmistress in the Post Office across the street.
He'd let his boys wander around smoking cigars,
tied them both to the porch as his babysitter.

Later I got to know him as a real gentle giant,
when one quiet purple and blue evening
he waved me over to his truck to chat,
parked all alone down there by the dock.

He knew that I knew that when a lobsterman,
with his traps all hauled out up in his yard,
comes down to sit alone for hours watching
the Southwest Chop roiling up the Western Way

and the mist tiptoeing up the Acadia mountains,
like so many tough old Cranberry men of the sea
who came there before him, he must be very sick
and his Spirit will soon rest deep in those waters.

We chatted about things, even joked a little.
I know he felt better—though we had shared
his secret with only a few kind words and a smile.

DRIVING DOWN *THE AIRLINE*

Maine Rte. 9e runs down east from Bangor

The Airline winds along on a huge esker,
our last great glacier's deep river of stone,
where a mile of ice wore down a mile of slate
before plants and animals crept back in.

You wind like a snake through the ice
as you drift through the land on the air,
sway back and forth with the breeze,
and float up and down on green waves.

The *Old Ones'* villages and houses are gone
but treehouses play high up in the trees.
Ancient maple stumps circle like Stonehenge.
Rotting walls lean together like praying hands.

Quiet loggers and their horses are gone forever
and huge log trucks and saws roar in the woods.
Gray ghosts of cedars wave out of the heath.
Mosquitoes and *no-see-ums* sing to fly-fishers.

Huge B-52s fly due east-west out of Bangor,
practicing low bombing through the bare beauty
of gray granite nubbles bobbing all around them.
Pilots from the Great War still smile and wave.

DEER CAMP

I've found my own perfect peace
reading a little poetry just before dawn—
watching first light creep over the Heath
to set the frizzled tamaracks on fire

—in deer's black eyes shining under dawn halos
of yellow birch and church spires of black alder,
which grow in my city of multi-colored apple trees
which roll like Christmas lights down 5th Avenue,

perfect peace coming back late to camp,
cold and wet and dirty, to laugh and joke,
overeat and overdrink by a crackling fire,
with my proud *Swamp Yankee* friends

frying up fresh deer heart, liver and onions,
partridge and cusk in garlic and butter,
warming up fall's thick black bear stew,
blueberry pie picked out back last summer

having a few beers, and a few beers more,
dreaming our Coyote Moon trickster myths,
Tim sitting around all week by the firebox
playing solitaire in his *brown-spot* underwear

tales of brotherly love, jokes and puns,
and bragging about *the one that got away,*
told over again and again so many times
as the years smiled slowly by.

Ice Fishing Dreams

We all loved the sheer immensity
of Moosehead Lake in mid-January,
huddling under south facing cliffs
to shelter from a fierce *blue norther*

bellowing well down below zero around us—
rib-eyes, red hot dogs, homemade sausages,
deer steaks and bear meat from the fall,
even the occasional fish we caught

shining, deeply gorgeous, gloriously black
winter nights, the darkest I've ever known,
lying on my back looking at up the sea of stars
showering down from my infinite night ocean

feeling all the excitement captured
in the taut bodies and intense stares
of tropical fishermen peering down
in Picasso's *Night Fishing in the Antibes.*

Checking my lines at night for delicious
prehistoric-looking bottom-dwelling cusk,
which looked like they had just emerged
from the depths of the Continental Shelf

our snow-blind line of dancing snowmobiles
coming up just short of deep open water
one night, where we would have launched
ourselves over the dam into *Ice Fishing Heaven*

then finding our way home by dead reckoning,
before GPS, then laughing and joking about it all
over and over, down through the years.

Something Wrong
on Maine's Back Roads

***** A Big Old House *****

Dust whispers in the curtains
under the high peaked roof
—the breeze from a punched out
back kitchen window?
—bugs waffling in the dark?
—newborn mice, or bats?
or the little old lady who hasn't
been seen since Fall?

***** A Playground *****

A swing set so splayed and sunken,
its rusty seats sit on the ground.
A few old tree house boards
flitter in a dead apple tree.
A little red wagon is only red rust,
its handle a sharp splintered palm.
A plastic doll waves its only hand.

***** Black Rot *****

So many roofs recline under
funeral shrouds of blue plastic
that may run all the way
down to the ground,
lasting for only a few years
over the moist black rot,
before wind and rain
rip it all slowly asunder.

A Hug in the Snow

The weatherman on the radio was saying:

I've never seen it like this!
It's blowing sideways outside my window!
It's raining and sleeting and snowing,
all at the same time! —and it was.

Just south of Bangor, a Mom and Dad
were driving fast up to BIA
to see their son come home from Iraq—
six days early, on one hour's notice.

As the four-wheel drift started,
his Mom barely had time to scream
We're going to crash!
as he listened horrified on the cell phone
a Maine Troop Greeter had given him.

Bangor is in the Great State of Maine,
Where Life is Worth Living—
so even before the rollover was over,
cars were stopped in both lanes,
and before the first teardrop fell,
she was on her way north again.

But the giant troop transport
was already waiting
in line for take-off,
a huge gray steaming beast
with deep red flashing eyes.

Then all of a sudden,
her son walked down
the ramp into the lounge,

gave her an enormous
three-minute hug

turned and saluted the crowd,
waved once and was gone,
even before the cheers
and the tears, and the waves
of rhythmic clapping started.

—a random act of human kindness?
—the new American patriotism?
—the infinite grace of God?
—a Maine wink and a smile?

All of the above!
and a single phone call
from a tall man in blue
with a 9 mm. pistol on his belt

and a huge .357 magnum
in his shoulder holster,
who quietly watches everything
and truly believes his job is

To Protect and Serve

WORLD ENOUGH AND TIME

We could spend a lifetime
watching the Universe
grow from singularity
into a luminous egg

the strings of black holes'
fury vibrating the surety
of eleven dimensions
of mathematical purity.

We could hear the
pinwheel galaxies howl,
watch a trillion stars
in each one prowl

winking on and off
like fireflies—
eons of event horizons
twinkling in our eyes.

Or we could just lie
in the garden and think,
smile as the suns sets
in sky blue pink

and the Moon rises high
on the Back Shore.

FLOWERS ON THE SEA

How would I remember her in Eternity,
were I the one casting flowers on the sea
for my little *SEAL* baby, lost on Pan Am
Flight 800, in the waves off East Moriches?

—tiny starfish hands clasped in golden balls
as she was born into my arms
the window seat where we read
Good night Room and *Goodnight Moon*

the time she shouted out so loud
Red-light! Red-light! Red-light!
when a strange tower appeared
on Mount Waldo one night.

I'd remember her in storm surge
and sea smoke on the Back Shore,
where she found the graptolite fossil
I'd been looking for all of my life

the little bunny in the blue dress
that she tucked into my arms, to
keep me safe in the strange hospital,
and that will always watch over me

how she loved our Penobscot point,
power spot of *The Red Paint People,*
where we found the ancient Indian
carving and watched the osprey soar

and that she wrote: *If Peace were a forest, we'd all
sway together with the trees. If Peace were the fog,
trust and friendship would seep into our lives.*

LIFE'S BEAUTIFUL BORNING

LIFE'S BEAUTIFUL BORNING

I. Life's Beautiful Borning
             as spoken to history by Black Elk—*heyoka*
             and *wachasa wachon* of the Oglala Sioux

Great Spirit dreamed everything
as hoops within hoops—
white wings, buffalo and man
all in worshipping groups.

Great Spirit dreamed all
worlds happy and free,
circles within circles 'round
a great flowering tree.

Forever and forever
he loved all living things.
Two legs and four legs,
wings, fins and roots

stars, birds and spirits
all danced in one loop,
with Twelve Moons
and Four Horses
in Spotted Eagle's swoop.

II. Childhood Visioning

When I was a baby, a long flat dark cloud
whispered sweet nothings to me out loud.
The grass grew so green, the Sun was so bright,
the birds were all singing—everything was right.

Then when I was a little boy my body bloated.
My mind slept tight while my spirit free-floated.
The Six Grandfathers gave me a flowering stick,
chanting my life's mission was to heal the sick.

A cup filled with waters from our world foredoomed
sang also that our lifelong fight for peace also loomed—
my mission to shine bright sunlight on our last hopes,
then lead fallen warriors off Death's slippery slopes.

As big boys we played the wide days into twilight,
young warriors on our ponies first learning to fight.
Loose rumors of war's scorching foreboding plight
echoed our war whoops down canyons' deep night.

III. A Time of Troubles Coming
Wasichu—a whiteman

Two men shot down
from a swift little cloud,
then turned into arrows
that thundered out loud:

Evil gnawing Wasichus are
coming on iron roads
to crush The People under
unbearable loads.

The Flowering Tree will
wither under the sky.
Medicine spirits and
healing potions will die.

The wind will be fiercer,
the snow fall so deep,
your families in square gray
houses will starve and weep.

Lightning will strike your
rainbow tepees roofed with clouds.
Your lives and your culture
will lie under funeral shrouds.

In a crooked gulch, butchered
women will lie scattered,
while your starving children
wander hungry and tattered.

IV. Death of the Beautiful Dream

Wasichus swung smoking,
whirling, cackling guns
and our screaming horses
turned with the wounded to run.

Swarms of moaning butterflies
came fluttering 'round,
while The People in webs
cowered deep underground.

Brother and sister four-legs
were scattered far and wide,
and the buffalo were all gone,
slaughtered just for their hide.

Measles and whooping cough
would not be tamed,
so Mad Dogs of Death
in our bodies were blamed.

V. A Frozen Road

Our culture with Wasichus'
could never blend,
so our *Red Road* at their
Black Road came to an end.

Some signed a pact with
Three Stars to live in their pens,
but our little band would
not eat their lies.

We wandered north
into Badlands' winters
where forever ends,
rather than wither
thin and insane

in Wasichus' prisons
for our honor and brains—
if need be to freeze
out on the buffalos'
vast northern plains.

VI. White Buffalo Calf Woman is Born Again

Now I sit in high hills of old age
while a bright future glistens
and I know from my visions
that the Universe still listens.

Broken smoking hoops
 circle up where it all began.
Four colored horses end-dance
the Fourth Age of Man.

Though my tears still run
with my deep guilt and shame,
that my failures may have
dishonored Black Elk's name

the voice in my head is again
a loud drumming—
White Buffalo Calf Woman
born again, is coming.

Though Great Spirit still
sleeps on bloody snow,
all the Star Nations on Earth
will soon proudly glow.

Thunder Beings in clouds
of all colors are bringing
peace pipes for all the World's
peoples and singing.

HEYOKA CLOWNS

sacred fools/empaths of the Lakota Sioux

We beg and cry out from our fools' tawdry dance
in empathic entanglement with all of Life's trance.
We shout and smirk back at Joy's sidewise glance,
put wisdom and balance back into Life's romance.

We're often born breech in both joy and pain,
sometimes talk backward as we try to explain
the answers to questions so deep in our brains,
why rich is not happy and glamour insane.

We have but one horn in our two innermost places
and only one mirror to reflect back on other faces,
in the infinite regression of both time and space
that forms the vision for Life's healing grace.

We hear Thunder Beings sing high in the clouds.
Our eyes joke back if Death moans too loud.
We'll cry your eyes out if you get too proud,
laugh and tickle you out of a funeral shroud.

In dirty torn clown clothes, sweat drenches our sores.
We sense other empaths sweeping up our feelings,
think ourselves out of our boxes, find peace in wars,
know hate comes entangled in true love's reeling.

Our halos are black and our shadows are white,
as we stumble and fall through the ballet of Life.
Our boundaries are horizons far out of sight
and new days will dawn out of our deepest night.

Winter Rain in the Desert

The sky is a dark grey circus tent
and over the sullen hills are bent
wrinkled thick-skinned clouds,
like gnarled old men on elephants.

Over the lone and level sands
black Devil's Tower stands,
controlling the ranks and files
of all its surrounding lands.

Our Once
and Future River
restoration of Maine's historic Penobscot River

In olden days the Penobscot was a waking dream,
with a coral reef's abundance of life and diversity.
Vast spring migrations of river life mirrored
plaintive callings of geese and ducks overhead.

Salmon returning magically from Arctic seas
spawned in silence and privacy all the way
from the Narramissic River, Marsh Stream,
and Sunkhaze Meadows to glacial kettles and tarns.

Ten-foot sturgeon cruised by on red October days.
A billion tiny elvers set out to find their way home
from eggs on the sinking vortices of the Sargasso Sea.
Uncountable alewives surged silver in small streams.

Then for several neglectful generations
the river choked and steamed brown—
a stinking cadaver of industrial shame.
They winked and snickered and no kid swam.

Now our new Bucksport Bridge smiles up again
at Mount Katahdin's shimmering *blue northers*
and back down on the golden lily pad of Sun
we see cupping the islands of Blue Hill Bay.

Shad and stripers now cavort well beyond Bangor,
while pink petals of *shadblow* float on the wind
like plum blossoms in ancient Chinese poetry.
The People of the Dawn return to sleep and dream.

SALMON HOMING

How do they home at the end of their numbered days,
across the Great Blue Oceans' rolling highways,
from Arctic dreamtimes halfway 'round the Earth
to find their final solace in the waters of their birth?

Their deep brains first find their fondest dreams,
mineral smells of seeping ledge and musky tree,
imprinted so deeply in dormant neural memories,
to help find again their once and future universe.

The polarized light of the Sun that lies
so deep in the green fire of their eyes,
wakes the dappled Moon that proudly smiles
down on all their journeys' driven miles.

Then the lateral lines paired on their sides
sing their magnetic songs across the tides.
Their eyes walk with Orion up into the sky,
to the Weeping Pleides to set their compass by.

Deeply scoured ocean paths of glaciers guide
them into the Penobscot's southward glide,
while the angled rays of a *thickafog* red sun
chant that their final journey's almost done.

At last, their ancient shining Auroral dreams
pull them back upriver into their natal streams,
into the deeper graveled coolness flowing forth
from more darkly shaded branches to the north.

DON JUAN'S LAND
after Carlos Casteneda

This is a lost land of mystic powers,
controlled fury and strange flowers,
where death stalks always at your back,
rustling down deep in the tiniest crack.

Here all good men are glowing eggs
and cacti walk quickly on little legs.
Coyote plays sly tricks on you.
A crow may be someone you know.

Old men float like astronauts in space,
laughing in your face as they float down,
only enchanted tentacles of grace
holding their bellies to the ground.

A warrior must always be on guard
for every little step in Life is hard.
Mushroom Spirits rule a mineral world,
make our minds like dry grass swirl.

Here one day, on High Eagle's perch,
you'll dance your last dance on the Earth,
as your soul like smoke in rainbows swirls
down through the crack between the worlds.

But if you follow The Path with Heart,
your mind and soul will never part.
Eternal Springtime's whispering showers
will bring an infinity of fluttering flowers.

DREAMTIME DOWN UNDER

I. Songlines
Aboriginal visions

The Ancestors sang the whole Universe
up into their beings from nothingness first.
The Dreamtime is both now and then—
forever in Forever, then forever again.

Everything still traces back all the way
to the singing dawn of the First Day,
when Songlines made the harsh desert soften
into plants and animals, landforms and men.

Our landforms still echo the First Creation,
birthed in the Ancestors' seething conflation.
Flailing magnetic sweeps of kangaroos' tails
blew little hills up out of the flatlands' trails.

Witchety Dreamings in underground tracks
filled up with water running off their backs.
Willy-Willy Winds danced in sunlit streams
of life in the sugar-bushes' deep dark dreams.

Phosphenes danced in the tribes' retinal spaces
paralleling matter and energy dancing in place,
patterning the meanings of their first written traces,
etching them in stone and bark like thoughts in lace.

The Guardians hover over ritual lands' blooming,
desert life's breeding and Devils' Tower's grooming.
Life's codexed genes still sleep deep in the Earth,
in seeds awaiting underground spiritual rebirth.

II. Every Day Dreaming

The Dreamtime still lives in flint-scraped stones
and crouching spirits in red-ochred pointing bones.
The Dreamtime still sings silent running songs
to rainbow serpents sleeping in deep billabongs.

Digeridoo moan deep deserts' sweet sounds,
echoing eternity in perseveratory rounds.
Bandicoots, wallabies and blue-tongued skinks
light up in deep greens and psychedelic pinks.

Eel-catfish glow, spawning in deep desert sinks,
while Ibis look up, guzzling sweet-watered drinks.
The Aurora still sweeps high in our widest skies.
Thunder weeps, showers fall and water seeps.

Willy Willy winds still dance in sunlit streams
deep in black magic cacti's deep dark dreams.
Witchety Dreamings deep in underground tracts
still fill as clear water seeps down their backs.

Bushtucker lifelines for the Tribes still thrive
in conkerberry, morinda, blue tongue and wongi;
quandong, kutjera, warrigal, and wattleseed damper;
in witchety grubs, honey ants, kangaroo and emu.

Our Aboriginal minds together still dance
as *Gubbaman* tries to enter into our trance.
Their sad lost empires try hard to subdue us
but our Songlines are still there to renew us.

III. Seas of Blood

Inverse cultural tides come in perpetual flood
and our hearts swim dreaming in seas of blood.
Our totemic souls strengthen with a fierce cry
as the *gubba men* try to bring the End Times nigh,

In skies over Tiwi, Kiranna and Arnhelm Land
naked men and women living in roaming bands
see storm clouds lowering, lightning brightening—
kangaroo, goanna, and kookaburra frightening.

Our highest chiefs are all on *Walkabout* teaching,
touching and talking, chanting and beseeching
with coolamongs, pitis, and digging sticks preaching—
with spears, axes, clubs and boomerangs outreaching.

Totem animals down from deep skis are falling.
Dead and un-dead up from below are crawling.
The Ancestors' Ancestors too are already calling
in auroras', comets', and bright meteors' spalling

using astral projection beyond the speed of light,
shaman's clairvoyance and remote-viewing sight,
dances, chants, spells, and kangaroo bone pointing,
our deepest thoughts with body paint anointing

Space-Time's dark matter and energy beaming
in unconscious parallel nether-world dreaming.
Now we sit in talking circles of the Ancestors' lives,
our souls singing with them in their stomach of sky.

Origin and Fate
of the Universe
I serve but One God – both chapter and verse –

and so it begins

First I danced in the melody of celestial strings,
a single thought dreaming in the mind of God,
born streaming through His Magic Hoop of Fire,
to the deep beating of His cosmic drums,
and joyous chanting of His Angels' Choir.

I lit up the first colossal blue-white stars' dance,
then collapsed them after but my briefest glance,
to explode as super-novae, their lives well spent—
exhaled great clouds of dusty death in foul breath,
to create carbon and metals for Life's first chance.

Planets formed from frozen gas and meteor scree,
and everywhere Life jumped up and twinkled on,
sometimes deep in a planet's warm shallow sea,
high up in flaming clouds of sulfur and ammonia
or crushed in the depths of a planet's deep freeze.

Everywhere Life still climbs the cliffs of Space,
forever seeking to find a new life-friendly place
to live when its own star eventually disintegrates.
Even now my *Great Inflation* has started returning,
and Mass eventually will flee itself faster than light.

Light's wavelengths become inestimably longer,
as I accelerate *Dark Energy's* harsh push-pulling.
As entropy grows ever more insatiably stronger,
galaxies now flying apart will someday no longer
see even each other's last gasping and squirming.

Soon I'll start to wink off my most joyous suns.
Even the supermassive neutron stars that live
cuddled up in some giant galaxies' loving arms
will explode and dissipate into infinite space
as leptons, bosons, gluons, quarks and strings.

As my great cosmic expansion ever quickens,
event horizons will become ever more narrow
at the infinitely small tip of Spacetime's Arrow.
Strings split even smaller than the Planck length
will have strange and charmed quarks' strength.

But my eternally foredestined dash into Forever
will be but the briefest and most blessed flash
between the twin poles of my cosmic gleaming
and the amazing lightness of being streaming
back into the nothingness of eternal dreaming.

All of the Universe's Higgs bosons, singularities
and split strings, in quantum entanglement
with God's next thought are still quite content,
to be just one small part of a charmed quark,
to live and die and live forever and ever again.

Then with all the glory of His infinite power,
I'll merge Heaven's ethereal clouds into buds
set to flower in latter times of His multiverse,
as He sets up Time's Arrow to wax and wane
at all the crossings of His fluttering branes.

   —and so it begins

ICE ON FIRE

39 / Ice on Fire

BUNNY

Under the faraway eyes of Abe Lincoln,
I tiptoed at last, alone in October
into the valley of the shadow of Death,
by the black wall where millions come,
but the loudest shout is a whisper.

On every stone shining there
in the moonlight, little spiders
were our soldiers' spirits
rappelling down silken cords

to protect their fallen brothers
who live in the nacreous gleam.
Little spider spirits were hanging
like strange fruit on silken crosses

to honor our heroes who jumped
from the *Jolly Green Giants,*
each one yelling *I'm Spartacus!*
into the furious face of the Sun.

As I flew home at last past the
Washington Monument, and over
the Memorial's black sword
plowed so deeply into the Earth

like a crashed stealth bomber
or an ancient symbol of death,
I was so glad I had touched his name,
though I didn't really know him

and only knew of him that his family
still loved him and still called him *Bunny*
and his unit still calls him *Griff.*

B-17 FLYING FORTRESS

It startled me in silver—a B-17 parked
so incongruously on the runway
by the Bar Harbor Airport Road

shinier than anything manmade
except maybe a telescope mirror
or sun-motes dancing on an August sea.

The ultimate Flying Fortress of its day,
its wings surprisingly short and stubby,
the B-17 was a strangely primitive toy

compared to the gray ghosts of death
that ride in our missile frigate fleets,
and the black wickedness of *Stealth Bombers.*

Its five fearsome machine gun turrets
looked like a small child's first fish tank,
but each one held a live human target.

I saw the silver stars my parents saw—
that so many of *The Greatest Generation*
followed across a strange and savage sea

from red dirt farms and Appalachian hollows,
Hell's Kitchen and Purple Mountain's Majesty—
so many lost in the silence of free fall.

THE WAY WE GET BY

The Maine Troop Greeters meet
our troops returning from combat

We thank you with smiling eyes that roam
back to your families huddled at home.
On strangers' cell phones your deepest fears
can start their healing in star-spangled tears.

Thank you for sliding on burning ice flares
through the black nights of your souls,
for patrolling daily through public squares
where bodies are smashed up fruit in bowls.

Thank you for diving through rings of fire,
dancing with new legs on steel stilts' gyre,
then walking stark deserts of phantom pain
without your face and half your brain

for smiling at friends from *punji pits* peering,
scratching out Death's eyes in treetops leering,
for watching children on fire pleading—
just one moment of slow silence needing.

And thank you for loving your buddies
through your own *thousand-yard stare*,
though your sleep will be torn up forever—
Death screams reeling in rockets' red glare.

ASK ME NO QUESTIONS

May 11, 2011 raid on Osama bin Laden

You packed your khakis and camos,
wore the dark blue silky USA t-shirt
you always wore when you travelled,
played with the kids for two hours,
then sauntered down the stairs

and gave me that great big strong
hug and kiss, just like always,
then the great big full arm wave
from your little red sports car.

I always tried never to imagine
where you went *on business*,
but I did of course know that
you *worked for the government*

and that our official agreement,
that dark night we gave our hearts
and souls to each other forever,
was *Ask me no questions
and I'll tell you no lies.*

Of course we both new
that we both knew
that we both knew
what you do.

I saw the great big shiny black car
with the thick shiny black windows,
drive up with the little American flags
saluting me from the front fenders

and instantly fell into my tears
when I saw your two best buddies
get out in full-dress uniforms
I had never even seen before.

They saluted and gave me
those great big long swaying
Thank You! and *We're so sorry!* hugs,
as their tears mixed with mine.

The stars and stripes
in their tears said
*Ask us no questions
and we'll tell you no lies.*

Three hours later the President
came on national TV and told us
where you all were today.

His eyes filled with tears
for *Seal Team 6*,
even though we all know
there is no such thing

as *Seal Team 6*.

Jessica Comes Home from Iraq

Shut your eyes now Jessica, lay your head back.
You'll be wrapped in the flag of America soon.
Your whole country saw you on TV, slapped
by a dirty little coward swathed in black

a little American woman with broken bones.
Our *Rainbow Warriors* are coming out of the
night to chopper you home in eerie green light
and a warm cocoon of American star foam.

You fought like a tiger 'til your ammo was gone,
then watched your whole unit get blown away.
Even the fiercest pacifists are proud of your
presence and courage in battle that day.

Shut your eyes now Jessica, in your little nest,
still bent and broken but unbowed.
You were someone's little baby once.
Now you've made your whole nation proud.

MY TWILIGHT LIFE

My twilight first sings of all beautiful things—
how I fought my way back with my sharp eagle's beak
and bright angels' wings, through all the wide days
with so much love for my country so far, far away.

A lead door slams down on my sweet sunset,
dripping blood clouds down through my trees,
choking and strangling me back into my past.
Night crushes me back down into Hell at last.

I crawl on my knees through memory's shrouds,
as surges of slime worms rise up once again—
creeping and crawling silently under my door
from my deep brain's dark rotting jungle floor.

They're wooing and cooing, cawing and pawing,
giggling and sniggling, sweating and petting,
saluting then polluting, purring then burrowing,
hugging then buggering, nurturing then butchering,

Now I hide all day long in my little hometown,
in my own little bed—puking over and over
in seething dread, and I drown every night
in the smirks that come down in the dark

from a c/o that still lurks up there on my bedstead.
I'm gagging and snaggling while our Lady of Liberty
and her Spirit of Justice lie silently there beside me,
shot in the head by a lying bureaucracy of living dead.

Hibakusha Hiroshima

Survivors – thought radioactive – were shunned

light of a million suns
slashes a hole in our
thin silk scarf of sky

thick black rain until morning
swims into our mouths
from vases on our graves

blood red morning sky breaks
on bodies clothed only
in blisters of black soot

one arm still holds
the strap in the streetcar
broiled bodies swim on the floor

swollen tongues eat death's shrieks
eyes hanging out on the floor
can't see our screams

burned bones and memories
her baby's head in a pail
fire behind them

a dead baby suckles
her mother's breast
even as both lay dying

skin hangs down in velvet sheets
where once a face with lips
and eyes had lived

legs swollen like logs
sludge up rivers dripping flesh
from shrieking undead

skin bleeding onto her hands
she finds strength to die
on her father's sword

Hell jumps out of our sins
cancers wake up from within
slowly we die

frozen breath swirls
over the front teeth of death
into our last flatness

brown bag Hiroshima face
one big central eye
still stares out smiling

No Worse Enemy
09/11/01

A young man with a perfect life
is driving home early one morning,
when black smoke bubbles up
and the Spirit of Fire enters his soul.

He comes in with a *thousand-mile stare,*
waves once on his way to the bathroom,
comes back out with his head shaved
and tells his wife he is rejoining his unit.

Half a year and half a world away,
his patrol stops two men in a fleeing car
filled with RPGs, AK-47s and IEDs
and holds them there for the MPs.

Some mumbling gibberish erupts
and they turn on him simultaneously.
His finger twitches instinctively,
as it has been trained so well to do.

A whole clip of his AR-15 gone in a flash,
he empties another one into their car,
kicks out the headlights and tail lights
and punches out all the windows.

He spray-paints the doors
the windows and the roof
No Better friend—No Worse Enemy!
The Spirit of Fire leaves his soul.

He salutes and kneels down to pray.

NEW HOPE FOR PTSD
computer guided visual imagery

A screaming still comes across the sky
from children on fire, running blind,
and the softest click of an opening door
can still throw me berserk onto the floor.

Soft rustling leaves deep in punji pits
still snap at me with sharp poison sticks.
I can still blow up a balloon of blue steel
that tastes like it's my last Earthly meal.

Back in 'Nam peace only came to me
hiding in full camos high up in a tree,
impassively staring in full moonlight
with my loaded rife and infrared sight.

I still sometimes swim crumpled up in bed
in my inner sea of mumbling, floating heads,
but now new virtual realities in cyberspace
help me fold my mind back into melded grace.

Slowly we dial up my most terrifying scene,
walk my mind slowly into the big screen,
find the fiercest dread in my deepest brain,
terror that still writhes in my infinite pain.

When the first tears come and the sweat drips,
my skeleton starts dancing and my heart flips,
my partner and I dial it back down 'til we see
my brain-rotting fungal dreams starting to flee.

1-800-THE-LOST

America's Most Wanted

My life's work is my shrine for Adam, my son.
They cut off his fingers and even his face,
kicked his skull around on cold barren ground—
that and his blood still the sole evidence trace.

Though we'll never take down the very last *perp*,
I'll be crawling the land searching endlessly 'round,
'til we take the very last child murderer down
and the last of the World's lost children is found.

On TV though once shy, in my cold bare warehouse
and brown leather jacket I'll forever seek exposure—
walk down their *Death Valleys* in the shadow of *Earp,*
where just finding remains will give someone closure.

All parents now know, though our work is searing,
my team and I will live always by our solemn vow—
to be there for them always, and to comfort and care
for all the wrent souls that we don't yet even know.

Still I sleep very well, each mission my first—
one less family with a child undead cursed.
I'll rope them in, my own worst of the worst,
hogtie them in the Sun and watch them burst.

And if my own little boy blue is yet to be found
after the next thousand scumbags get taken down,
I'll lie naked in Times Square for a shot to the head,
just to hold him tight in my very own arms once again.

BURNING SHIELD
the Jason Schechterle story

Courage is the handsome young policeman,
his patrol car rear-ended into a ball of fire
and his face seared beyond recognition,
alive only because a fire truck happened by.

Courage was making his mangled legs walk,
then run ever so painfully on the treadmill,
so he could carry the Olympic Torch of Duty,
Honor and Triumph as it came through town.

Courage is his beautiful young wife
still hugging him and kissing him
on the scar tissue that was his lips,
as they play with their little boy

the infinite love and gentle
dignity of his body language,
as his son shimmers
in broken colors before him

in his one good eye and says
You're not my daddy!
That's my daddy!
—pointing at their family picture.

Courage is his transcendent inner smile,
because he is still alive with his family,
and doing his work with his buddies,
though his face will never move again.

OUR LADY OF PEACE

She walks down a Greek road lined
with men crucified by the Romans,
each one screaming *I'm Spartacus.*

She camps with the blue and the gray
at Appomattox fifty years later,
now hugging and weeping together

sharing common pasts and futures—
their duty, their honor and their country
once again all one and the same.

She crawls with Japanese and Americans
out of the radioactive bones of Hiroshima—
the black rain of burns, scars and cancers.

She breathes in with a man
running a marathon,
then an Iron Man Triathlon

just to prove beyond the shadow
of a doubt that he is still tough
enough to rejoin his unit.

She cries with a Mom and Dad
so long after the flash of the IED,
watching their little girl so proudly

as she learns to walk again for them,
then ride her bike with her new legs.
They remember together her first steps.

911 REDUX

Firemen still float in their bunks,
dancing on the wings of the angels,
holding hands with the jumpers,
trying all night to pull them out
of the soft September breeze.

Police still sit silent in their cruisers,
eating donuts and drinking coffee
with old friends no longer there.
A plane flies in low over La Guardia
and trigger fingers still twitch.

A mom and dad come in with their kids,
bringing borrowed books back for others.
The librarian looks down at her list
of so many books, so long overdue.

Leaves swirl up in the Fall breeze,
and people reach for handkerchiefs,
squint and start to run a few steps
as a silent tornado of dust comes
around the corners of their minds.

Subway Ends—Everyone Must Exit Here
a red, white and blue sign cackles.
No one stands near the edge
watching the third rail anymore.

Our red, white and blue tears

will not stop.

LIFE IN A JAR: SENDLER'S LIST

a nurse who carried children
out of the Warsaw Ghetto

She tottered alone for so many years,
doddered out loud and swallowed her fears,
her life warmed only by the shuddering cries
of near three thousand little Jewish lives.

Her snippy little dog's bulging mucusy eyes
and her sweaty work stench, let her steal away
from the blood-caked claws and swastikas' lies
on the spotless uniforms of the *Übermensch.*

She coughed out loud and walked upwind,
grunting and jingling her tools in time
with her little babies whimpering cries,
drugged and dozing in her officer's cart.

Some of them probably even knew it,
then hailed the *Führer* all the louder,
trying to dream themselves back
again into her brighter skies.

Courageous landsmen spirited them away
to feed and shelter, teach and play.
She hid their names in a little glass jar
buried out back under her little apple tree

so the ashes of families gassed and burned alive,
could bring their spirits home again someday,
leave the bad dreams and atrocities behind,
live together again as one big happy family.

THE LITTLE BOY IN SHORT PANTS

The little boy in short pants raises his hands.
His shudder still travels around the world.
Waffen SS helmets and guns dance behind him.
Please put your clothes and valuables into one big bag.

His shudder still travels around the world.
Our great train of hope will bring your new life.
Please put your clothes and valuables into one big bag.
His mother fluffs his hair and says not to worry.

Our great train of hope will bring your new life.
Two lines four abreast march into history.
His mother fluffs his hair and says not to worry.
Shuttered cattle cars lurch forward in locked step.

Two lines four abreast march into history.
A huge gate opens up wide to greet them.
Shuttered cattle cars lurch forward in locked step.
Jolly *Oopah* music dances them out into the sun.

A huge gate opens up wide to greet them.
Bodies and feces writhe on the floor.
Jolly *Oompah* music dances them out into the sun.
Please put all your little bundles onto these piles.

Bodies and feces writhe on the floor.
Now take your clothes off to shower for a new life.
Please put all your little bundles onto these piles.
Now take in a deep breath for the future.

Now take your clothes off to shower for a new life.
The whole World pretends not to notice.
Now take in a deep breath for the future.
The little boy in short pants raises his hands.

SKY BLUE MIND

59 / Sky Blue Mind

REFLECTING THEIR ABSENCE

The 911 Ground Zero Memorial

Deep in the footprints of September,
where so many jumped out of the flames
and into the tears of the angels,
my fingers are touching the names

where the red, white and yellow roses
grow so deep into the black brass—
as the four colored horses of our
new American apocalypse.

Our hearts lie down on their hearts—
of children and friends and lovers.
Their eyes look up into our eyes
and our eyes cry down into theirs

from the deepest well
of the infinite regression,
of hope within grief
within hope within grief

the presence of presence
in the absence of absence,
in the dark falling waters
where our country rises up

once again.

SULLY

208 seconds, 155 lives

I blinked as the thin black line
of frenzied Canada Geese
danced on the far horizon,
then exploded on my windshield

—thuds and screams from Hell,
then the echoing silence
of angels in deep space.
My eyes flicked down

to the instrument panels—
both engines stalled,
altitude 2200, speed 250,
direction due north.

The map I built in my head
every day for forty years
shimmered before my eyes,
flashing with every airport

within a hundred miles—
the day's runway traffic
and holding patterns,
wind speed and direction.

Can you make it to Teterboro?
No! I'm landing on the Hudson.

I leaned hard left over
the twin towers of the
George Washington Bridge,
speed just above stall, then into

the pocket of boats opening up like
a baseball glove on the hand of God—
saw 911 already on the way,
even before we hit the water.

I walked the aisles twice
through the rising waters,
looking for the injured
and the terrified, then out

into the line of passengers
moving so slowly, quietly
and comfortably off the wing
into the arms of strangers.

The dreams and the sweats
are fading now.
I can comfortably retire,
and my family is smiling again.

They don't even ask why
I'm going back to work,
because they know

It's what I do.

I Want to Go to Space

Dr. Laurel Clark — Space Shuttle Columbia

When you were a little girl
snuggled with your Mom
on the sofa, you heard
One small step for a man—
One giant leap for mankind

—saw Apollo 13 splash down safely
after so many systems crashed—
because Jim Lovell said to his crew
and every expert known to Houston

Let's Just work the problem
over and over and over again
while they circled the Moon!

As a woman, you had *the right stuff*
to dance on the pillar of fire,
your immaculate soul hurled
into the infinite wilderness of sky,
in a brief shower of stars and foam.

But in all the glory of space,
even as you burned up
in the white heat of re-entry,
all you ever wanted to do
was *Just work the problem.*

After the crash your husband Jon
and thousands of volunteers
walked the land and sifted the soil
to put the shuttle back together,
so shredded families

could put shredded souls
back together again,
and lay them to rest
under sacred green lawns
all across the Heartland.

At your funeral Jon told us
about a little blonde boy
who had obsessed for months,
that his Mom would follow
Christa's shining path to the stars,

but couldn't remember crying
that day, when the whole World
watched seven pale white angels
ride in formation across the cold
blue skies of West, Texas.

Then as we readied you
for your final mission
the little boy said:

Mom, I want to go to space!
but don't worry
We'll Just work the problem

Together

No Better Friend
09/11/01

A young man with a perfect life
kisses his wife goodbye
and tells her to give the kids
a great big hug and his smile

clicks the cell phone off
and steps out into the perfect
powder blue September sky,
so glad he had looked into

his little girl's deep blue ocean eyes
and kissed her doll's forehead—
that he had promised his little boy
they'd play catch again that afternoon.

He is so glad he told his wife
to raise the children strong and true,
to know joy again with someone,
for her sake, and for his sake too,

to remember his name always,
like women who come to The Wall
to meet with their first loves,
married and happy again.

He hears the stones whispering
and the angels singing, as the ground
swirls up out of the long soft tunnel
of great white light and peace.

Awakening

Oliver Sacks *Ruth R.*
a 1918 pandemic flu victim

She was at the top of the World
when she went to bed one night in 1918,
but besieged by phantasmagoric fever dreams
of a frozen future which swept through her—
fear, dread, sweats, and un-localizable pain.

By morning she was a sentient statue,
frozen like one of Michelangelo's *Slaves*
struggling to erupt from a marble block,
water-boarded in a castle in the castle of herself—
her deep brain in the Black Hole of her Soul

mirrors reflecting off mirrors off mirrors.
A thought starting as a single point on a map
on a map, disappeared as soon as she saw it.
She slept wide awake but frozen for 43 years,
until the dawning of a new *Magic Potion*—L-dopa.

She erupted like a long dormant volcano—
smiling and dancing and flying, happy
and free. She talked of her youth with an
incandescent nostalgia for sights and smells,
though strangely separated from the newsreel

of all her later years flashing by. But soon she
started to fall back into the endless echolalia
lurking at all the event horizons of her mind,
her death spiral winding inside her life spiral—
forever back into her night of the living dead.

DYSLEXIA

Reading could have taken Gina a lifetime of tears.
She rubbed her brittle fingernails on tiny smudges
until the little letters danced together on the pages,
then held little bird feet down on their new stages.

Then some began to join together as syllables,
obeying secret laws of self-assembly in her eyes.
She fought to pull meanings from the cryptic smiles
of words scrambling around in their new cages.

She joined words as sentences, to coalesce and play,
rife with gaggles of unknown meanings of our new day.
While everyone else saw words' meanings in their eyes,
she saw words as butterflies fluttering in higher skies.

It won't take another lifetime of hard work and tears
for Gina to harvest just a little of all the stark beauty
of mankind's history living in so many bountiful ages.
The world of ideas already flocks over her inner sea.

JUST LISTEN TO THE PATIENT

After five minutes in the ER you should know:
Sick or well? Admit or send home? OR or ICU?
STAT tests or refer now? Live or die?
Will we know before they leave the ER?

I've been on the Internet and I think I have—

Take them very seriously and get
the best science you can get—
from anyone, anywhere, even the book
waiting on the front seat of your car.

They'll at least be a little relieved
if they don't have it, but even if they do,
with a little human comfort and caring,
a few simple tests and a good referral.

But if they are never sick,
even with the strangest complaint,
you'd better be very, very sure it's nothing
before you just write a prescription:

I feel like my head is going to fall off!
because it is! The rheumatoid arthritis
has eaten away the odontoid process, the last
little bone holding her skull onto her spine.

It may still take an hour to ask all the questions,
look and listen, feel and smell, review results,
do the paperwork for a good medical record,
make phone calls—and dictate drivel for billing,

but you won't be disappointed and neither will they.

GLORY OF THE HUMAN SPIRIT

She was there waiting for the hospital elevator
in thin gray pants and a tight pink-purple t-shirt—
her nurses' aide trailing a few feet behind her,
smiling and patient, but ready—as were we all.

Her whole body writhed slowly right before us,
up through her back and her neck, her face and
fingers tremoring and her arms flapping a little,
as if climbing her own DNA double spiral staircase.

Her frozen mid-torso leaned far over to the right
but her right hip ticked under her even further,
like a pendulum, but still she walked so proudly,
with 2- or 3-inch steps at maybe 8 per minute.

She hugged her little black purse so closely tucked
under her arm, so tightly held with her little fingers
Her smile twisted up and around it like a coiled snake,
or a fullback diving in high over the goal line.

Though her twinkly eyes could barely look up
over it and out at us, she still smiled up at us.
She moved her lips and the tears ran down—
a hello? an apology? a dream? a thank you?

—crawling the last few feet of a marathon?
—about to be born from a dying mother?
Just happy to be alive in this wonderful world
and in the next one—coming for her soon.

BLACK IRIS OF THE BLACK PLACE

Abiquiu—Georgia O'Keefe's *Ghost Ranch Garden*

She is still the black iris of the *Black Place*.
Her artistic immensity and painterly grace,
the intensity of her mind and soul still trace
millennial smiles onto her weathered face.

Pistils and stamens still rub in the secret bowers
of her erotically re-curved fairy-fountain flowers,
love lasting forever in her secret soul windows,
weaving volumes and curves, light and shadows.

In later years, as her keen eyesight slowly faded,
structures without visionary colors she traded,
so sculptures' subtler interior life forms invaded,
Ghost Ranch Garden's visionary's death serenaded.

Her clam shells morphed into mountain ranges
as she herself morphed with all Life's changes,
needing ever more infinite cognitive space
to compensate for her true love's lost face.

Shaman's spirits still worship on bended knees
in the layered fossil rainbows in her ancient seas—
in the wind-polished skulls, antlers and pelves
that hover over her stark skeletal ghostly trees.

Dazzling desert sunlight on the wind still scours
the gorgeous gaggles of her perennial flowers.
Mares' tails and cirrus clouds' fine floating faces
still lower on *Pedernal's* thunder-clouded towers.

AN OLD RED CAPE COD

A cute little red and yellow Cape Cod
still sits lonely atop a little rise of red—
last Fall's burned off blueberry fields.

A bib of yellow and blue perennials
and escaped exotics sweeps up
her smooth green dress of lawn.

A scarlet oak grows bravely up through
a flattened stone wall and some huge old
rusty barrel hoops from an ancient brewery.

Pink granite foundation blocks lean forward,
frazzled mortar squeezing out from between.
A purple cherry tree's mourning cloak hovers.

A green splurge of sunlit fields and weeds
shines through the windowless living room.
The front steps and doorway are long gone

but somebody still keeps the lawn mowed.

A Cold Day in November

She kisses his casket and lights the eternal flame.
The little boy in suit shorts salutes his father.
Cronkite lifts his glasses and the World cries.
A rider-less horse rears up and down in fury.

The little boy in suit shorts salutes his father.
Tears shine through his mother's black veil.
A rider-less horse rears up and down in fury.
Boots backwards in the stirrups face the future.

Tears shine through his mother's black veil.
His red blood still runs down her pink dress.
Boots backward in the stirrups face the future.
The empty saddle waits for our new leader.

His red blood still runs down her pink dress.
Canons of war and peace sing down the Mall.
The empty saddle waits for our new leader.
She kisses his casket and lights the eternal flame.

MISSING MAN FORMATION

to my wife- awaiting my heart transplant

The mists of the meadow in our darkling eyes
gathered our souls up in North Carolina skies.
I climbed in your window from the fireflies' mist.
Love and friendship enveloped our very first tryst.

Warm tides of love tugged us up Eggemoggin Reach,
and pheromones leaped from our deep pelvic bones.
We dreamed up our baby one night on Castine Beach.
One bright January morning we snuggled her home.

Bed boats! and *red lights!* danced through our days—
Drag me around on the floor, Dad! in Fall's deep haze.
Beauty on beauty rolled out of her childhood's maze,
but sudden on sudden our ships' souls were ablaze.

My heart fled away in immune conflagration—
one heart and three souls in *missing man formation.*
My medicines tore us all apart while I gaggled.
Our nerves snaggled up and our two hearts haggled.

It's been a long fight through so many a long night,
but my new heart thrives to our passionate delight.
The rage is now dying, bright colors are flying,
my spirit there for you forever, or I'll die trying.

Now it's time together to slowly grow old,
and never again let the craziness take hold—
in afternoons' gloaming let the smiling sun in,
once again by the fireplace lie skin to skin.

Then softly growing calmer, quieter and whole,
cuddle again under thick covers, soul to soul.

NAMASTE FOR VICTOR

The island sends me with their love for you,
eyes glinting sky blue on white sheets in ICU.
Calm crystal tide pools before Rooster Club met
pull your spirit back from the brink even yet.

As a little boy on the shore you chose your fate—
to fish the sea of life, not sit onshore and cut bait,
to hunker down on the nets for weeks and wait,
to fish from dawn to dusk on Life's lonely straight.

With beaked nose, floppy ears and leathery skin,
you worshipped the Sun all your salty years—
such an amazingly strong, thin and gnarly man,
smiling even as you floated over so many fears.

I leave you now in white-sheeted repose,
in the Ocean's love as Time's Arrow goes,
so proud of the blue star life you chose
on Grand Banks' ever-circling windrows.

Your eyes now mist over in waves' foggy lee,
to dance forever in the Sun on a following sea.
We'll all be there together to bless your soul
in our little white island church ceremony

then we'll all walk with you to the cemetery,
the women all in fluffy white flowered dresses
their mothers and grandmothers sewed,
men in the same black suit from the old days.

A WALK IN THE CLOUDS

Out of my dream-bright window
I climb the moonbeam stairs,
touching the little stars' shadows
while they dance in pairs.

Night owls stare at the musky sky,
craning their necks in silent rows,
amazed to see me floating by
without my clothes.

All around my tiny town
people snuggle in peaceful homes,
while fluffy snow drifts down
in our magnificent glass dome.

High above Earth's filmy shrouds,
I wave to my friends below,
stirring the moon-be-dappled
clouds with my big toe.

Then glowing like a speck of light
in the Universe's sea of foam,
I float on my back, a tethered kite
and reel myself back home.

LOVE

A peacocks colored wheel
of eyes clambers up
my pentimento skies

pearlescent paints of intrigue
punch through our walls
of wildflower dreaming

my ache of seeds spills
into your bed's dry petals
a new life sings

slightly aslant we all grow
into our yellow bird
of inner sun

nostalgia for the infinite
sleeps deep in our
garnet of dreams

WHEN DEATH COMES

When death comes, I want to
be able to step boldly through
the crack between the worlds,
knowing already what it's like

to lift up the edge of the sky,
float through and drift forever,
cradled in the loving embrace
of immaculate white light

see my spirit floating
free as thistledown
with all my dear friends
on the dawn wind of space.

I want to look upon all of my life
as rainbows and thunder,
and see Eternity in the
blinking of God's eye

and I will remember
each of my friends
as rare and as singular
as a nocturnal flower

each of my loved ones as a fruit
picked at the peak of ripeness—
an angel fallen preciously
down onto the Earth.

And when it's all over
I want to be able to say

All of my life I rode
the whirlwinds of amazement,
taking the whole Universe
into my soul.

I don't want to wonder
if I've made of my life
something useful and real,
or find myself frightened

and sighing and wondering
why I had never fully inhaled

such an amazing world.

ABOUT ATMOSPHERE PRESS

Atmosphere Press is an independent full-service publisher for books in genres ranging from non-fiction to fiction to poetry, with a special emphasis on being an author-friendly approach to the challenges of getting a book into the world. Learn more about what we do at atmospherepress.com.

We encourage you to check out some of Atmosphere's latest releases, which are available at Amazon.com, BarnesandNoble.com, and via order from your local bookstore:

Ghost Sentence, poems by Mary Flanagan

That Scarlett Bacon, a picture book by Mark Johnson

That Beautiful Season, a novel by Sandra Fox Murphy

What I Cannot Abandon, poems by William Guest

Such a Nice Girl, a novel by Carol St. John

Makani and the Tiki Mikis, a picture book by Kosta
    Gregory

What Outlives Us, poems by Larry Levy

How Not to Sell, nonfiction by Rashad Daoudi

All the Dead Are Holy, poems by Larry Levy

Bello the Cello, a picture book by Dennis Mathew

Rescripting the Workplace, nonfiction by Pam Boyd

Surviving Mother, a novella by Gwen Head

Winter Park, a novel by Graham Guest

In Gratitude to My Parents

My father Averill arrived at Ellis Island as a little 8year old Jewish boy fleeing the Nazis with just the clothes on his back. He worked his way through CCNY and Yale Medical School, was a varsity swimmer and almost made the US Olympic Team in fencing.

He became a Lieutenant Colonel in the US Army Medical Corps in the Pacific Theater during WW II. He was lead pathologist on The *Atomic Bomb Casualty Commission*, documented in his book *Encounter with Disaster*. Thirty years later he went back to Germany with the US Army civilian protocol rank of Second Star General.

He was widely loved as an outstandingly skilled and caring teacher of students from their first year in medical school to internationally known academic physicians. The *Liebow Auditorium* at UCSD School of Medicine is named in his honor.

My mother Carolyn made it all possible. She grew up in Southwest Harbor, a tiny Maine seacoast town and was Valedictorian of her Pemetic High School class of 13. She volunteered on Pearl Harbor Day and became a Captain in the US Army Nursing Corps—in my Dad's Yale Unit.

When she returned home from the war, she took off her Army uniform forever, like so many brilliant and talented women leaders of her day. She raised 3 boys strong and true in a loving home in rural Connecticut, and in our summer home on Great Cranberry Island.

ABOUT THE POET

For forty years, Paul Liebow and his family have lived on the Penobscot River, just upriver from Bucksport's Saint Regis Paper Mill. His original property deed included *salmon weir rights on the Penobscot*. Paul is a board-certified ER doc with a lifelong dedication to emergency medicine and a broad spectrum of environmental issues.

He is a prolific writer of op eds and Letters to the Editor on medical and environmental and political topics. He was Maine Region 4 EMS Medical Director for 20+ years and helped write the first Maine EMS Emergency Medical Protocols and guidelines.

He wrote his hospital's first Hospital Disaster Plan. He was the Citizen Representative on the Maine Legislative Commission to Rewrite Maine's Disaster Protocols after 911, which were adopted unanimously by the Maine Legislature.

In later life, and after a successful heart transplant, he began to express his knowledge and life experiences through the introspection and vision of poetry.

CPSIA information can be obtained
at www.ICGtesting.com
Printed in the USA
FSHW011735120519
58075FS

9 781645 166764